Raga for What Comes Next

poems by
Dianne Borsenik

STUBBORN MULE PRESS
DEVIL'S ELBOW, MO

Stubborn Mule Press
Devil's Elbow, MO
stubbornmulepress.com

All poems copyright © 2019 Dianne Borsenik

First Edition 11 7 5 3 2 1
ISBN: 978-1-946642-93-6
LCCN: 2018967936
Design, edits and layout: Jeanette Powers
stubbornmulepress@gmail.com @stubbornmulepress
Cover Image: Jon Lee Grafton
Title Page Image: Dianne Borsenik
Author Photo: John Burroughs

All rights reserved. No part of this publication may be reproduced or transmitted in any form or by any means, electronic or mechanical, including photocopying, recording or by info retrieval system, w/out prior written permission from the author. Brief passages quoted for review purposes are permitted.

more praise for:
Raga for What Comes Next

Dianne Borsenik's *Raga for What Comes Next* offers a framework of poems that burn with wit and wisdom. We learn to rely on the improvisational style of these poems: their turns, their moments between moments where — upon a closer look — empty is not so empty. Even a discarded bottle has "a shaft of sunlight" to refill it. Borsenik shows us how we all have an "unspooling of identity," both individually and as a community. But she also reminds us — with sharp imagery and musical riffs that lift from the page — that we return to ourselves and must wait for what comes next. Fortunately, we don't have to wait in the unknown alone. We have these poems — that sing with music, art, and pop-culture — to show us the joy, beauty, and fun that exists in our waiting.
—Nicole Robinson

Musical and mystical, often in the same poem, Dianne Borsenik has penned a series of bluesy ragas full of moons, Quentin Tarantino, hot rods, mass murders, dust, the Dog Star, the Weather Channel, and us as "paper lotuses," cross-stitched with a series of precise ekphrastic poems derived from different forms of art. This is a book that moves easily between forms and worlds, sometimes with full declarative clarity, sometimes in more opaque lines that resist easy explanation. For in the end, this is a book of celebration, for language, for life, for all that can be seen and unseen: "This is the music of love. Grandsons, / morning raga. Grandfather, evening raga. / Maybe *waiting* is just a word for the raga / that plays in between."
—Sean Thomas Dougherty, author of
The Second O of Sorrow

Ragas, jazz, Dylan, Björk, oxygen, Japanese legends, Lennon, McCartney, origami, Tarantino, Michelle Obama. I could go on in listing the inspirations Borsenik provides, tied together in four parts, each one an instrument that contributes to the rhythms. From the sitar to the tabla, the poems read like a double album, one you will play many times, finding something new with each listen. As Borsenik concludes, "the *real* prize is not knowing."
—Puma Perl, poet, author of *Retrograde*, recipient
of the 2016 Acker Award for Writing

In this magical, musically-inspired collections of poems, Dianne Borsenik carves thoughts and orchestrates observations with the precision of a master. From seeing Scooby-Doo in a rust fragment to musing on shocking deaths imposed by man and nature, she strips away pretense and predictability. And in the end, Borsenik proves that while "sometimes, ordinary / isn't near enough," her pungent words are more than enough to reshape and refurbish the head space you occupy.
—Christine Howey, Executive Director of Literary Cleveland, writer/actor, *Exact Change*

Dear reader, if you have come to these pages for sweet tales and harmonious endings, then you have come to the wrong place. Dianne Borsenik has a penchant for tart language, a luscious way with metaphor, and is not above making outright rowdy proclamations. "I'll barefoot the rails / after they've cooled"... "go full-throat / full-throttle, head high and balls out." Every line of this *improvisation* of texture, taste, sound and smell is Dianne Borsenik, laid bare, then gathered, framed and hung out so the sun shines all over it, "a radical art form...a special breathtaking."
—Kari Gunter-Seymour, author of *Serving*, Poet Laureate, Athens, Ohio

Dianne Borsenik's *Raga For What Comes Next* really is a raga: improvisations from set patterns. Through kinetic, metaphor-crackling couplets, ekphrastic poems that blow the frame off the genre, and reverberations of her rock 'n' roll influences, she makes a ringing music both delicate and terrible; as in her poem *Tides* that weaves political slogans, the Greek god of dread, and the gracious power of natural phenomenon to create what comes next, "At the crest, / one wave merged / from many, resolute."
—Ray McNiece, author of *Our Way of Life* and the forthcoming *New Haiku*

I have been enjoying the poetry immensely ... I started plowing through Sitar... then went back and read things slowly and digestively... more often than not I found a sequence of words would stop me and I would think "Oh, my... this belongs in a song"... or find myself daydreaming a whole storyline from that snippet. It is truly an excellent, excellent work ... full of insight, passion and humor combined with the integrity of a poet who celebrates the human condition with every syllable. BRAVO!
—Alex Bevan, singer/songwriter, "Skinny Little Boy from Cleveland Ohio"

Raga: a melodic framework for improvisation

Much gratitude to Jeanette Powers, Jason Ryberg, and Stubborn Mule Press for this New Year's dream-come-true.

Thank you, James Borsenik,
for making my life a happy raga.
I love you with all my heart.

Contents

I. Sitar

The Color of Oxygen	10
The Same River Twice	11
Hagiography	12
Branches	13
Psalm to Deep Time	14
Train, Loud, Lonesome, Leaving Without Me	15
Sometimes, Ordinary	16
Sonar Readings	17
Churning Butter	18
Dust to Dust	19
Discovery Sutra	20
Grand Reflections	21

II. Shehnai

A Quotidian God	24
Orrery	25
Eclipsed	26
Paradigm for Unraveling	27
Tangled Up in Blues	28
Tears, Detachments	29
Day of the Dead	30
Scapular	31
Church of the Mind	32
Recycled	33
Deciduous	34
Linnea Quigley Hugs My Husband as Leaves Continue to Fall	35

III. Bansuri

Luminaria (Meditations Before Kaddish)	38
Realities in Totemic Flux	42
Women's World War	46
Tides	47
Illumination	48
La Familia	49
This Can't Be Oklahoma	50
Seeing Jim Morrison in Giant Eagle on the First Day of Autumn	51
Finding Myself Inside a Quentin Tarantino Movie in Cleveland at Four O' Clock in the Afternoon	52
Sitting Next to Paul McCartney in Bomba's One Week After the Autumnal Equinox	53
Paul Simon Sees Angels in the Architecture, But I See Scooby-Doo in a Flake of Rust	54

IV. Tabla

When You Read the Poems of the Dead	56
the close reading of poetry	57
Sutra for the Missing Monkey	59
Raga That Plays In Between	61
All That Jazz	62
When the Son of a Motherless Goat Tries to Stare You Down,	63
Evolution Mantra	64
Imagine	65
Homecoming	66
Discoveries in the Key of God	67
La Fiesta	69

I. Sitar

The sitar, a stringed instrument with a seasoned gourd for a body and a hollow wooden neck with movable, raised frets, has a sweet, overtone-rich texture. Stretched under the frets are a number of sympathetic, resonating strings.

The Color of Oxygen

> *"Singing is like a celebration of oxygen."* —Björk

Tree releases oxygen,
which becomes a raga.

Earth sings in tabla of thunder,
the bansuri of wind.

Birds pluck the strings, multi-tonic
melody in ascent, descent.

Each time it rains, another
improvisation blooms.

The Same River Twice
    —after "Songs Inside" by Isabel Farnsworth
    —after Heraclitus

The face you show the world.
The face you show yourself.

Looking forward, knowing change.
Looking back, what's done is done.

All those voices looped like fortunes
inside our heads, all those dreadlock

meditations escaping to reveal
the soft underbellies of our rivers,

slipping like blonde curls from
fingers, the unspooling of identity.

Hagiography

*Scientists have discovered a geometric object
at the heart of quantum physics that questions
time and space as components of reality.*

What is time, but an amber jewel
at the heart of a lonesome moon,

and what is space, but a hand
that anchors the moon in its place?

Scientists have no word for the color
of orgasm, or for the look of birds

arranged like musical notes on wires.
They have no memory of luminous

mysteries, only answers
to questions about reality

that I'd never thought to ask.

Branches

It's complicated,
all these branches of our past,
where and who we came from,
whose hair, whose eyes,
whose nose we have,
whether we were spawned
in oceans or fell like angels
from the sky. It's tangled
in half-truth and faulty memory,
mostly lost in the waves of time.

It's complicated,
all those branches snatching
at the wind with promises
of flowering and fruit,
the dendrite pattern
twinned in upside-down
relief, the mystery of samara
spinning out to find its now
and take root.

Psalm to Deep Time

"Birds are the only dinosaurs...still alive today."
—Michael Lee, evolutionary biologist

this
is what I
see with my
chambered heart:

from the cloud, rain
from the throat, canticle
from the hand, benediction

there is no outside
the world is a room

these are harmonics of time
these are your basilicas
enter and be unique

dinosaur knew
and found
his way
here

Train, Loud, Lonesome, Leaving Without Me

Concrete never kept me,
fences never held me back.

Wings are for wind,
hands for folding sunshine,

mouths for holding hearts.
The tattoo of wheels on tracks

clatters loud and lonesome
in someone else's story.

Me? I'll barefoot the rails
after they've cooled,

a balancing act of foolhardiness
and faith, caution left hanging

in the long morning, distant
whistle moonlighting as map.

Sometimes, Ordinary
    —after a true story told on a car show

Sometimes, ordinary
isn't near enough.
Sometimes, you need
a breath of whimsy,
a brush of the macabre,
to make you feel alive.
Sometimes, you need
to pluck out your glass eye,
roll it around on the table,
get it pinstriped by Von Hot Rod
just for the hell of it,
just because you can,
just because it's there.

Sonar Readings

Swim into indigo
to discover treasures
beneath the waves;
release voices
from tangled nets.
Earth's blood
is a hymn and you
must be saved,
baptized by its tide.
Wilderness awaits;
complete the journey.
Plumb the depths.
Look inside.
Get wet.

Churning Butter

How are we to hold on to butter,
and how are we to weave its blaze?

Churn days into moments, rupture
membranes between earth and sky,

and as sweet cream clouds release,
lick salty skin and rise on sunlight.

Dust to Dust

First, remove the cloak of doubt.
Strip yourself of discontent
and despair, wear only your skin.
You are meant to wrap yourself
in sunlight. Take yourself to a sacred
place and face the night. Burn sage,
burn away the demons that rob you
of your rightful place and peace,
burn incandescent bright
and release the ash into the wind.
Daub what is left onto your forehead
and cheekbones, own your defiance,
own your weaknesses and your age.

Remember you are fashioned
from dust and to dust you shall return—
but know that everything in between
can be glorious. Burn. Burn. Burn.

Discovery Sutra*

> *"Three things cannot be long hidden: the sun,
> the moon, and the truth."*—Buddha

Swim as though the river
is burnished with fire.

Swim through the rough
tangles of current, swim

against the siren call of
gentle moonlight, swim

with all your heart's desire
to the impossible Dragon

Gate and climb its stairs,
shouting with joy.

Discover that you are not
ordinary koi, but dragon.

---

*According to Japanese legend, if a koi succeeded in climbing the falls at a point called Dragon Gate on the Yellow River, it would be transformed into a dragon. Based on that legend, it became a symbol of perseverance in adversity and strength of purpose.

Grand Reflections
—after "Grand Reflection," 2017, oil on canvas,
by Lydia Owens

It's just Rayleigh scattering, you know, that blueness of sky, a vast, commonplace scattering of wavelengths, a spray of sunlight filtered through oxygen and nitrogen until it reaches our eyes (which also are not blue, but that's a story for a different day). Call it an optical effect, an illusion; there's no azure, sapphire, indigo dye involved, no pigment, no minerals. Pure blue, like the blue reflected in wrinkles of water, has a wavelength of four hundred and seventy nanometers. It's all very technical and sterile. The actual word *blue* comes from Old High German *Blao*. Blue is not among the first words assigned in a nascent language; often, it is one of the last colors to be named. A new synthetic blue, phthalocyanine, was created in 1930. Widely used in pigment, ink, and dye, it likely has become the basis for contemporary artists' bold brushstrokes behind wispy clouds. Cobalt blue painted the *Starry Night* behind a yellow moon. Scientists say the sky is not blue. Artists—and children—know better.

Earth wears her necklace of lapis lazuli blue and laughs.

II. Shehnai

The shehnai, a musical instrument similar to the oboe, is often used in temple ceremonies to create and maintain a sense of auspiciousness and sanctity.

A Quotidian God
> —after "Quotidian Gauge," cardboard, paper, string,
> by Julianne Edberg

Gauge me. Measure me.
Set me at gorgeous.
Set me at normal.
No.
I'm not normal.
Set me at gorgeous and sensitive.
No.
Set me at terrible and sensitive.
This is Old Testament.
Discuss.
No.
Set me at funky.
Set me at funky and ultrasensitive.
Set me at funky and ultrasensitive
for eight hours, then insipid and weak
for eight hours, then delicious, and, oh,
I don't know, pick one.
This is New Testament.
Gauge me. Measure me.
Nothing will be recorded, I promise.
Speak into the speaker.
Speak up.
Discuss.

Orrery*

Circles and ellipses
of orbits. The tilting of axis,
the specter of eclipse. Magnetic
poles. The way the continents look
from a distance. The blue of the oceans.
The giant red spot, a storm that never ends.
Alien ice on alien moons. Sterility. Loneliness.
The rise of the trilobites. Dinosaurs. A crater the size
of an extinction level event. Early Man. The Question:
Are we alone? The Answer: A billion, billion galaxies.
Möbius strip of time and energy. Where were you
yesterday? Tomorrow? Always, the relentless
revolutions. Gravity. The spinning of tales.
Orion. The Twins. The Dog Star and The
Bear. The Swan. Event horizons.
Decay of orbits. Each Man
dies so alone. The origami
of orrery, of living.

An orrery is a device showing the relative positions and motions of bodies in the solar system, driven by a clockwork mechanism, named after Charles Boyle, Earl of Orrery, who ordered the construction of the first one.

Eclipsed
—Thursday, October 23, 2014

missed
the eclipse
it slipped
a disc
whisper-
kissed
the sky
and dis-
appeared
a solar
whisker
will o'
the wisp

Paradigm for Unraveling

Morning is a backstory,
already shared;

afternoon lies,
threadbare and wanting,
on the garden bench.

The day unravels
a little at a time,

until all that's left
are the wings, hungry for
the canticle of wind,

but uncertain how
to go about finding it.

Tangled Up in Blues
—after the digital print "Tangled Up in Blue"
by Janet Mikolajczyk; song titles by Bob Dylan

It's all tangled, tangled,
strangled up in blue; in
previous beauty and broken
promises, it's never gonna
be the same again, paths of
victory and utopian memories
stained with azure, with
ultramarine; it's tangled,
tangled, mangled up by stones
rolling, hard rain falling, wind
blowing, no shelter from this
indigo storm, only desolation
between the sheets, times
a-changing in the streets. It's
all tangled, tangled, angled up
in blue, Willis-Tyndall scattering
the eye, Rayleigh scattering sea
and sky, the moon is blue,
the highway's blue, something's
burning blue; all I really want to
do is matter, find the Dream, end
the screaming. Oh, precious angel,
turn every grain of sand from blue,
farewell to Heaven's door, leave
that cobalt door alone, oh, oh,
ring them bells, give me one more
night, one more cup of coffee,
it's not dark yet; it's tangled,
tangled, jangled up in blue, written
in my soul, the weight, the shape
I'm in, and whatcha gonna do?
It's alright, it's all over now, baby—
I'm only bleeding blue.

Tears, Detachments*
    —*November 09, 2016*

Something sudden. Bursts
of shadow, likely trauma. Changes
allowing the brain a sharp corner.

Damage, loss. To shrink, to detach.
Time may thin, easier for scar to form.
Tears, breaks, holes occur.

Evaluate history, magnifying
areas of place. Waves of detachment.
Troubling left untreated.

Tears, blood, strands of light. Signals.
Serious changes, symptoms of
separates. The present, difficult.

Beneath the lift off, common growing.
Conditions pool, peripheral.
Best to follow recovery. Numbed,

seal around the freezing, resume
activities. Avoid filling the bubble. A need
to heal. Safe to socket; buckle in.

Done, stop. Prepare. Experience.
Recovery may be shield, limit, monitor.
Follow-up, gain. New eyes.

**an erasure poem, citing the booklet "Retinal Tears and Detachments,"*
Krames Patient Education, © 2003 The StayWell Company

Day of the Dead
    —*November 1, 2017*

There's a high wind warning for
Denver today, and the Weather Channel
is recalling an active hurricane season.

Puerto Rico and the U.S Virgin Islands
are still in ruins. A terrorist killed
eight yesterday in New York with

a rented truck, "You Can Do It, We
Can Help." A teacher in Strongsville,
Ohio, was murdered by her son-in-law

to be, and she was buried on what was
to have been her daughter's wedding day.
A couple that escaped the slaughter of

"58 dead and 489 injured in Las Vegas"
died two weeks later in a car crash,
less than a mile from their home. First

responders were at the neighborhood
crack house again yesterday morning.
There was frost last night. Something died.

Scapular
— *after a photograph in Casey Rearick's "Inference:*
Anxiety, Sensuality, Tension" series

Jutting outline of scapula,
geometry of muscles rising
to meet fire-branded hair;

you can almost see where
the wings were stripped away,
scars lost in skin the color

of summer cloud. Tension
cloaks the vertebrae,
worn like a commitment.

Church of the Mind

> One more climb up the too-steep stairs to the apartment, one final look around. Austere walls enclave the ghosts of holidays, passionate celebrations both cheerful and tearful. A tumble of flashes—get-togethers spanning four years' time—but nowhere to sit and remember. The refrigerator shelves are bare of food and drink; the cupboards over the sink are the next to be packed. The bathroom is spotless; it would be sacrilegious to flush the toilet and make sound in this holy place.
>
> all these boxes
> stuffed full of
> empty rooms

Recycled

Every time renters move out of the house next door, there's a jumble of things left behind on the tree lawn. Discarded items of a past life, no longer needed or useful. A broken desk chair. A lampshade sans lamp. Things scuffed and dull, abandoned to the elements, awaiting the hands of the junkman or waste management.

discarded bottle—
a shaft of sunlight
refills it

Deciduous
>—*after Mikola Gnisyuk's "People in Trees (The Rooks Have Arrived)," 1964*

The world has lost all color
here, between these sticks of trees,
in this broken, chiaroscuro day where
snow carpets the field, and the empty sky
never brightens past pale.

It's easy to imagine one person following the urge
to climb a white trunk, climb high and cling tightly,
keening with the northern wind and
offering sacrificial skin to the spirits of late fall.
It's easy to imagine one person joined by
two or three others, then an entire throng of
hadji seeking the blessings of their Mother Earth.

Eventually they'll drop, exhausted, like leaves,
walk away into the dusk and become human again.
Other spirits will call them to sleep.

But on this one day, in this neck of the woods,
deciduous desire transforms them, sweeps
away thought, transubstantiates flesh into foliage,
sanctions cryptic silhouette of rooks against the gray.

Linnea Quigley Hugs My Husband as Leaves Continue to Fall

Cinema Wasteland:
a gathering of tribes.
Character actors and horror
producers mix and match,
disciples convene. Oeuvres

outré, pseudo-sanguinary;
anything you want, anybody
you want to be, all-day
pass. The promissory note
of dressing in black.

Scream Queen puts her
arms around my husband,
tells him he's special. It's
been seventeen years
between; both older.

This October, another
uncommonly warm day.
Maple leaves continue
to suicide, a drive home
through liquid gold, beautiful.

III. Bansuri

The bansuri, a flute typically made of bamboo or reed, is associated with Lord Krishna, and represents the way the life force (*pran*, or literally, "breath") is converted into a musical resonance (*sur*).

Luminaria (Meditations Before Kaddish)

I

We are here,

fragile bits of starstuff
caught in this particular

spasm of time,

missing each other's
orbits by nanoseconds—

pushed together
by centrifugal forces,

pulled apart
by gravitational forces,

all of us traveling this
white river together.

II

All of us, together,
white lotus starstuff

carried down
this white river, swept

this way and that,
shoved against rocks,

forced apart
by circumstance,

and sometimes

returning to float
with each other

in a cosmic dance
of invisible currents.

III

We are here,
our souls lighting

the fragile paper
of our skins;
burning

with the flames
of a billion stars.

IV

When you hold
the flame in your hand,

you burn. There's no
turning back.

There never was.

V

We are here,

paper lotuses
folded, fingered,

freed
on white water.

Where we go
and how we drift

is up to
the peace we make

with the river.

VI

Water
and flame:

one cannot exist
without the other.

VII

Paper burns;
transmutes into ash.

Blue flame dies.
Ashes mix

with the river,
indistinguishable.

VIII

Capillaries of river
branch ever outward,

destinations
unmapped.

IX

Ribbons of flame
and the flow of the river—

never the same thing
twice.

X

We are here,

white lotus
luminaria

burning our way
downstream, all

these billion billion
lights drifting

on this white river
of stars, eternal,

spreading, stretching
as far as the I
can see.

Realities in Totemic Flux

Whose finger is this,
rising from
a chatoyant horizon
to anoint our foreheads
with sigils arabesque
and oneiric?
    A thousand
totems manifest.
Estival
    evenings
tremble, seismic
inquisition.
Sands, twitching,
    have turned into
conchitic signatures
spelling out
    storm
and genuflection,
canticles of axiom
and dichotomy.
Solstice skewers
loam,
dilutes viscid blood,
releases
    strange colors.
Subterranean aggression,
    blooming through
crucifixion of
    rainfall,
martyrs animus,
incarnates anima.
    Chills
ripple. Iconoclasm.
Diminutive spasms,
    whispering over
    the lake,

suggest minatory
vespers, alabaster bones
cast into protean mouths,
imminent twist
of condition.
Thunder recalls
consummation, heralds
fruiting, snapping of stalks,
pods, the breaking of
    steel shadows.
    Drop
deceits, the fiction
of science, the veils
between bonfire
and obsidian face
of night; we are Ouroboros
unblinking, and must
respond.
    Like song,
sparks wink into existence,
then diminish, disappear.
    From
horizon to horizon,
    the sky
swells; constellations burn.
From this,
    the sound
of divination. Reaping
    gilds
what comes after.
Holy, the pyx of my mouth,
the sacrament of
    my breath,
holy the dippers of gourd
and husk, holy the yield
and the yielding,
the immolation of saints.
    It's not
about gravity, perigee,

apogee, escape,
it's not
    how hard
the ground can be, nor
how eager
    the wind.
The catalyst is Time.
When the trumpet
    blows,
accept the sequelae
of harvesting,
chaff, fodder.
Respect the scythe,
the torque of inevitability,
    but
stay maverick.
Know
    that
    it does
not end with the
    scattering
of ashes, smudged
thumbprints of
    maple,
aspen, poplar, hickory,
oak.
Can't you feel
the cotyledons beating
their tiny
    wings
in your chest?
    On
the wall, the chart
is static. In nativity,
    its
analemma unknots,
appetite unslaked by
declination on its
    way

    to cheat
false communions.
This shall be
the true mystery:
a viridian
    death
anabiotic;
consecrated,
hallowed, beloved,
divine.

Women's World War
> —*after the photo "Women's March on Washington,
> January, 2017" by Joan Lederer*

Armed with posters and chants, the excited buzz
becoming louder as each new voice enters the fray,
covens of dreamers, these delegates, a united sex,
denimed, tie-dyed, long-skirted, calling for counterblow.

Enacted by change and refusal to compromise, *leitmotiv*
finds identity in their grandmothers' pasts, in a tableau
gone at once future and retro, prism and mist.

Here, the raised fist, the defiant eye, the smiles
inside the smiles, here, the solidarity and roar
juxtaposed with a general atmosphere of tranq.
Keepers of the faith, warriors determined to score coup:
Love, Love, Love Is All You Need to
move the earth with a pussy-capped master plan.

Tides

> *"When they go low, we go high."*
> —Michelle Obama

Beginnings, almost imperceptible.
    Neap tide, right angled astronomy,
  barely a ripple
        to expose the pulling away....

Gradually, a stronger undertow
    as solar and lunar gravities diverge.
  A more insistent tugging,
      a more insistent return,

conchitic signatures inscribed
    and erased, a fresh epistle each time.
  Without the power
      of geometry to slow

the surge, expansion of range,
    spring tide blurring practiced certainty
  into fuzzy aftermath.
      Now, here, new ribbons form

and coalesce on shifting shores.
    Neap tides swell into a rising, becoming.
  Breakers of change:
      struggle, renunciation;

acquiescence refused,
    heterogeneity embraced. At the crest,
  one wave merged
      from many, resolute.

Deimos, stripped of the power
    to scream, liturgy denied. Gravities
  diverge.
      Now, here—a spring tide, going high.

Illumination
    —after "Girls in the Garden" by Mary Ann Tipple

It was all about flowers that year,
peonies, forget-me-nots, daisies,

with petals to shred and promises
to keep. Fingers looped stems into

halos of color and perfume, before
finding other mischief to make.

What is the flower for awakening?

This quartet, casual in the portraiture,
captures knowing in their smiles, eyes

saturated with secrets, their youth
still wreathed in fabric blossoms.

By summer's end, the branding of
sunlight worn like carnival masks.

La Familia
> —*after the collage "La Familia" by Lisa Ortega*

Tradition, and history. These are the things
he carries within, beating where the heart should
be. The breath his mother gave him dances
in his chest, but he slides his hand into his pocket.
He will not respond to the music.

Cloud, and feather. These are the things
she carries within, and rain, and the urge to sway.
She binds her hair behind to keep it from danger.
Not a hair out of place. Her tiny breasts bloom,
knowing they've nourished.

History, asleep in the hollow. Tradition, afloat
on cerulean. His arm cradles nebulous, eventual,
an intention of tomorrows. Feather leans in, desire
to be closer. Rain in her movement. He will not
respond to the weather.

Tradition begets rooted as one, history begets shawl
and sandal. Cloud begets one foot slightly in front
of the other, desire to stray. Feather begets a held
hand, lest little become lost. Her father's insecurity.
Her mother's persistence.

This Can't Be Oklahoma
—after "Yoder Farm," watercolor on canvas,
by William David Simon

This can't be Oklahoma, not
this farm, so desolate, so sterile, so
barren of cow. This can't be Oklahoma,
where it's possible to see more
cows in one day than in one's
entire life outside Oklahoma—
coffee-colored, nut-brown cows,
cows in plenitude, cows ubiquitous.

This can't be Oklahoma, and
this can't be April, when the cattle
have calved and every blade of
viridescent grass is called into play
to pasture the cows, to nourish
the cows, to cradle the cows when they
tire of eating and fold their legs. There's
too much undisturbed grass for April.

No, this can't be Oklahoma, not
these whitewashed outbuildings
surely filled with pale ambient light
and the petrichor of the morning's rain,
dust sifting into empty corners. No
bellows, no snorts, no stamping hooves
inhabit here. This place, so *un-bovine*,
can't be Oklahoma.

Seeing Jim Morrison in Giant Eagle on the First Day of Autumn

It's the hottest it's been
on the first day of autumn
since 1895, and 92 degrees
Fahrenheit calls for ice
cream and alcohol

to celebrate. At the State
Liquor Agency in Giant Eagle,
Jim Morrison, reincarnated,
scans the bar code
on the bottle and tells me

to insert my chip. He
doesn't smile the entire
time; he just tosses back
a lock of hair and purses
those iconic lips.

I can't help myself. "Do you
know who The Doors are?"
I ask him, and he
meets my eyes. "I've
heard of them," he lies.

"You look like the lead
singer," I tell him, hoping
once home he'll Google it,
discover the music, see
for himself proof that

fifty years ago, he
walked the earth as a god,
wore black leather, sang
Come on, baby, light my fire,
ignited a generation.

Finding Myself Inside a Quentin Tarantino Movie in Cleveland at Four O'clock in the Afternoon

It's four o' clock in the afternoon, and we're the first ones through the door at Porco's Lounge and Tiki Room—at least, that's what we'd planned, but we're met by a man-bunned film crew setting up their gear. I sit in our

usual booth, order a Fogg Cutter. Wild surf music rips through the speakers—Dick Dale's "Misirlou"—and I can hear owner Stefan telling one of his stories, which then segues into an interview with *Destination Cleveland*.

I order another drink. It arrives, dry ice making it smoke and bubble like a witch's cauldron. The interview ends. Stefan saunters over to "Walk Don't Run," slams his wallet on the table. It's the one from *Pulp Fiction*—you know

the one, the Bad MF one—and everything turns surreal. All those little tiki-faced mugs bore into me with unblinking eyes. The skeleton that swings from the rafters swigs his never-ending string of LED light. The question WWDD—

What Would Don (the Beachcomber) Do—hangs over the bar, and the smell of Pusser's Rum is in the air. "Tequila" hits the speakers, and that's when I realize: I'm in a Quentin Tarantino movie, and my drink is ready for its close up.

Sitting Next to Paul McCartney in Bomba's One Week After the Autumnal Equinox

It's only been one week since the autumnal equinox,
but the weather has turned chilly enough for jackets.
We've just enjoyed a clambake, and I'm thirsty for
an adult beverage. We head to Bomba Tacos and Rum,
where I discover they carry Blackstrap and order a
Painkiller. It's dreary outside, beginning to rain,

and in walks Paul McCartney. Not the seventy-six
year old Paul McCartney, not the *Egypt Station*
Sir Paul McCartney, but the scruffy one from 1960, the one
who played skiffle in the German clubs. His hair is long
and shaggy, he's wearing jeans, and he has a bit of a beard
starting. He sits down on the barstool two seats from me

and orders a beer...a Budweiser, of all things. I sneak
another sidelong look. Yep, it's him, right here in Cleveland,
all time-traveled and magic. He's heavier in real life than
in photos I've seen. But there's the chin, and the eyes.
He looks weary, though, a little like he might have
an idea what's coming down the line, along with all

the success. The band's breakup, Lennon's death, and
Harrison's, those are big ones, sure, and the devastation
of Linda's disease. Good years there, and gone too soon.
But I think I can see other things in his face; maybe it's
future's ever-uncertainty: global climate change,
the incivility of politics, a new kind of polio, the everyday
waking to a world blown backward by gales of ignorance.

God knows, it's hard to walk against that kind of wind.

Paul Simon Sees Angels in the Architecture, But I See Scooby-Doo in a Flake of Rust

Paul Simon sings of "angels in the architecture,"
but I look down and see Scooby-Doo in a rust
fragment in the parking lot. That's the Rust Belt

for you, not a lot of looking at fancy buildings,
but a lot of watching where you step. Potholes,
broken sidewalks, small lakes from torrential

rainfall, the threats of unrestrained pit bulls
and tough guys with no regard for human life,
so many things to avoid—it's a must, focusing

your eyes and attention on where you're going,
instead of daydreaming about—or regretting—
where you've been. That's the Rust Belt for you,

a full-steam-ahead, eyes-on-the-prize, "I get
knocked down but I get up again" mindset; grit,
determination, and amusement in a flake of rust.

IV. Tabla

Tabla consists of a pair of drums played in various configurations to create a wide variety of complex sounds and rhythms. The intricate music of the drums reflects the rhythmic framework of the piece.

When You Read the Poems of the Dead
*—for Margie Shaheed, Maj Ragain, Christian O'Keeffe,
Russell Salamon, Bill Hurley and Jim Lang*

When you read the poems of the dead,

*don't call us dead, commemorated, worth
having, a responsibility, the hardcover collection,
a selection of ghosts, an appropriate prayer—*

When you read the poems of the dead,

*find the process necessary, remember, marvel
at the staggering array; we are just away, the latest
fascination, crossing the boundary between—*

When you read the poems of the dead,

*call us powerful, meaningful, what we are
to each other, inaugural, living, a radical art form,
the perfect distillation, a special breathtaking.*

the close reading of poetry*
—for Alex Gildzen

multiple words

elisions likely
          occurred
     regularly
in latin

aural likeness of sound
sound that can be utilized

the implied
the strict
dictionary definition of a word

the concept of using
        historically / dialect
        technically / immediate application

              living languages
often used in poetry

      others
      entirely
      made of

vanishing
      vanishing
           syllables

   disemvowelment

the concept of using
      <u
        sing>
    inevitable

   the
      skips
   the
      dropping

*A found poem during a Google search for "when a poet skips vowels in a word." In literary criticism, close reading is the careful, sustained interpretation of a brief passage of a text. A close reading emphasizes the single and the particular over the general, effected by close attention to individual words, the syntax, and the order in which the sentences unfold ideas, as the reader scans the line of text. — Wikipedia

Sutra for the Missing Monkey

Share comfortable silences…but communicate.
Escape expectations; exceed your environment.
Establish rapport. And boundaries.
Nullify doubt; it can drain you.
Own the skin you're in.
Explore your sulci and gyri.
Vanish into the Om.
Ignorance is not an excuse.
Leave the door open. Let it be.

Humor is a precious resource.
Energy—positive and negative—wells from within.
Allow yourself time to breathe.
Relish the extant moment.
Nothing can prepare you for what comes next.
Open your heart to possibilities.
Enter through the exit; exit through the entrance.
Variety is the vitamin of life.
Is this where you want to be right now?
Lennon had it right: *imagine*.

Smile, from the soul, out.
Pause before you act.
Effective dialogue can enlighten.
Ask yourself, *is it worth it?*
Knowledge is power; use it.
No one really knows what you're thinking.
One word can start—or stop—a war.
Even bodhisattvas make mistakes.
Voice your concerns and deal with them.
Ill will may occur nonetheless.
Love yourself. And love love.

Dig deep for answers.
Occam's razor may be applied.
Never give up.

Operate at "full speed ahead."
Easy is not always best.
Venture into something that scares you.
Intent is good. Doing is better.
Look. Listen. Laugh. Learn.

Raga That Plays In Between

So much of life is spent in waiting,
waiting for the right time to come
around, for things to go your way.
Waiting for the next paycheck.
Waiting in line. Waiting your turn.
Waiting by yourself.
Waiting to hear your name called.
Waiting to learn the results.
Waiting on someone while at work.
Waiting with someone at bedside.
Waiting for the person you love,
waiting for new life to be born.

My friend Bharat tells me one of his
grandsons is named Ahir, a Hindi word
describing a classical raga played in the
morning. He tells me his most recent
grandson is named Sahan, after a
classical raga played in the evening.
This is the music of love. Grandsons,
morning raga. Grandfather, evening raga.
Maybe *waiting* is just a word for the raga
that plays in between.

All That Jazz

Aging population resolves to keep its jazz,
becomes a congress of gray matter plus Gray Panther: sly
camouflage of colorful scarves and comfortable spandex,
delegates tuned in, turned on, outrageous and outlaw,
edges honed by experience sharper than a shiv,
fueled variously by weed, beef, tequila, and tofu.

Generational shockwave, this Baby Boomer cohort:
hippies, Spinners, classic rockers, thrashers,
iconoclasts questioning authority and parameter,
jaded marchers protesting political tranq,
keepers of faith, experimenters, change and shakeup,
lovers ever-seeking a bigger O,
monument to yesterday. Tomorrow's hymn.

When the Son of a Motherless Goat Tries to Stare You Down,

don't blink.
Don't even think of giving him the satisfaction
of a cowed reaction; don't little-down
yourself for a clown who's living in the past
century. Dismiss his attempts at intimidation,
ignore his dictatorial oration.
He's out-classed and can be out-sassed.

When the son of a motherless goat
tries to silence you, go full-throat,
full-throttle, head high and balls out,
bubble-pop his ego, Jericho his walls.
Let him stomp, let him stew, let him pout.
He may think he's God's greatest creation,
but he can't touch you.

When the son of a motherless goat
tries to get your goat,
don't let him. He isn't worth the hassle, not
for one minute. Stun him with indifference,
let him wonder at your grit.
Grin at his impotence. Don't grovel, float.
You've got this. Win.

Evolution Mantra
—with thanks to Sean Connery in The Rock *for line 18*

Thoughts for the day:
Here's where it starts—with me.
Each moment holds delicious promise.
Revisit the past but prepare for the future.
Envision evolution;
See change as opportunity.
Believe in yourself as a force to be reckoned with.
Evolution is the solution to
Ennui and stasis.
Never give up;
Anything can happen.
Center yourself and carry on.
Here's where it starts—with me.
Anger is counterproductive;
Negativity is restrictive.
Goal-orientation is the key.
Eclipse yesterday's accomplishments;
Only pussies whine about doing their best.
Failure is not an option.
Here's where it starts—with me.
Enter the keystroke and
Activate the future.
Realize revolution and evolve.
Thoughts for the day: Here's where it starts—

Imagine
>—John Lennon d. 12-08-80
>—John Glenn d. 12-08-16
>"Zero G and I feel fine."

Imagine
a night filled
with a billion stars,
and all of them
beckoning,

each fleck
a canticle
in the cathedral
of the cosmos.
Imagine

the black
aisles between
the galaxies as holy,
as paths,
as pyx

holding
the sacrament.
Imagine communing
with time itself:
each second,

each tick,
brimming with
the same luminous dust
as the stars.
Imagine.

Homecoming
—after "Hampuy" by Catherine Joslyn, fabric and paint
("Come back to the place where you always belonged")

where the moon spirals out of control
across a sky smitten with the eyes of time
where leaves mask the intentions of trees
where the serpents transubstantiate
into streamers of celebration
where shadows distill patterns
from the design between breaths
where horizons spill secrets
where your hair brushes my chest
where your hands perform a conjuring
where old walls dissolve into themselves
nothing more than strata of color
where you return, at last, to yourself
come back with me to this place
where you've always belonged

Discoveries in the Key of God

What note resonates
on the cusp
of arcane revelation?
    Morning
has crystallized
into a spear
plunged through glass,
    has broken
holiness into atonalities
punctuated
by hallelujahs.
    The window
blinks, only for an instant.
Who will deliver us?
    Razor shards
amplify the descant,
inexhaustible
and organic. Oracles,
    scintillating,
    relinquish
results of their scrying
to anima, animus,
the calyx of heart,
    perfection.
Splinters
    work their way
out, an exodus. Pray,
O Diaspora, pray
for the lucent cartography
    under skin.
    Don't wait
for the congregation to dissolve.
Resolution lies
in disjunction. Pray
    for the alarm
to sound. Be gong, or

tiniest
vibration in the ethereal
    clock. Even
    the moon knows
    when it's time.
Enough. Awaken. We need
    to go.

La Fiesta

What comes next
in this Cracker Jack® box
of life?

The *real* prize
is not knowing.

Acknowledgments

Grateful acknowledgment is given to the following publications in which these poems first appeared, sometimes in a slightly different form.

A Rustling and Waking Within — Branches
Akitsu Quarterly — Church of the Mind
Chiron Review — Hagiography, The Same River Twice, Illumination
Common Threads — Orrery
Conclave: The Trickster's Song — La Familia
Dirty Chai — Dust to Dust
Gasconade Review — This Can't Be Oklahoma, Seeing Jim Morrison…, Finding Myself Inside…
Great Lakes Review — Churning Butter, Evolution Mantra
GTK Creative Journal — Deciduous
Houston & Nomadic Voices Magazine — Discoveries in the Key of God
Main Street Rag — When You Read the Poems of the Dead, Grand Reflections
Poems-For-All #1650 (2017) — the haiku "discarded bottle" in Recycled
Survival: a poets speak anthology (Beatlick Press & Jules' Poetry Playhouse Publications, 2018) — Tides
Recession in Neverland (Paladin Knight Publishing, 2017) — Paradigm for Unraveling
Resist Much Obey Little: Inaugural Poems to the Resistance (Spuyten Duyvil, 2017) — Tears, Detachments
The Offbeat — Eclipsed; Sometimes, Ordinary

48th Street Press Broadside Series — Sonar Readings, The Color of Oxygen
Spare Change Press, 2013 — Luminaria (Meditations Before Kaddish) (as Luminaria)
The Cranky Pressman/Lit Youngstown — Train, Loud, Lonesome, Leaving Without Me

Author's Note:

Realities in Totemic Flux and Discoveries in the Key of God contain separate, nested poems within them. The titles of the hidden poems are Perfect Storm and Party's Over.

Dianne Borsenik is active in the northern Ohio poetry scene, and travels to perform her work throughout the Midwest. Her poems have appeared in numerous journals and anthologies, including *Rosebud*, *Slipstream*, *Chiron Review*, *Main Street Rag*, *Lilliput Review*, *Modern Haiku*, *The Magnetic Poetry® Book of Poetry* (Workman Publishing, 1997), and *A Rustling and Waking Within* (OPA, 2017). Crisis Chronicles Press published her first full-length collection, *Age of Aquarius*, in 2016. Actor Jonathan Frid ("Barnabas Collins," *Dark Shadows*) used three of her poems in his one-man touring show *Genesis of Evil*, and Lit Youngstown printed her poem "Disco" on their tee shirts, which makes her feel like a rock star. Borsenik is editor/publisher at NightBallet Press, and lives in Elyria, Ohio. Find her on Facebook and at www.dianneborsenik.com.

www.ingramcontent.com/pod-product-compliance
Lightning Source LLC
Chambersburg PA
CBHW030131100526
44591CB00009B/610

9781946642936